DAD JOKES

For Kids and Their Adults!

1000 Clean and Absurdly Lame Jokes that Will Crack Up the Entire Family!

CIEL PUBLISHING

"They're so bad that they're good..."

What are dad jokes?

The definition itself is an oxymoron. A dad joke is a joke that is not funny. For instance, do you remember a time when you heard a joke so lame that it made you laugh? Yup, that was probably a dad joke.

In this book, you will find an arsenal of these infamous jokes to throw around when you're with family or friends.

Like all jokes, they help break the ice and get amazing conversations started. In many occasions, popping out one of these during otherwise bland family dinners or get-togethers can make all the difference.

They also come with an added benefit for the young ones…

As counterintuitive as it sounds, dad jokes are great for expanding children's' vocabulary and flexibility in speech. The average dad joke is based on a play on words or on the use of puns. As a result, they're great tools for:

- Expanding on existing vocabulary
- Practicing homonyms (words that sound alike but have different meanings)
- Understanding homographs (words that are spelled the same but have different meanings).
- Connecting existing vocabulary with new, different contexts.
- And much, much, more!

I hope you're ready for this weirdly funny adventure!

Dad Jokes

1

Q: What kind of music is a balloon scared of?
A: Pop music.

2

Q; What do you call the security outside
of a Samsung Store?
A: Guardians of the Galaxy.

3

Q: What are the strongest days of the week?
A: Saturday and Sunday, the rest are week days.

4

Q: Why was the stadium so cold?
A: Because there were a lot of fans.

5

Q: Have you ever watched the movie
"Constipated"?
A: It hasn't come out yet.

Dad Jokes

6

Q: What did the seal with the broken arm say to the Polar bear?
A: Do not consume if seal is broken.

7

Q; Why do the French eat snails?
A: They don't like fast food.

8

Q: What do you call a bee that was born in the United States?
A: A USB.

9

Q: Where do animals go when their tails fall off?
A: The retail store.

10

Q: Why can't a bike stand up on its own?
A: Because it's two tired.

Dad Jokes

11

Q: Why did the beautiful girl throw the butter out of the window?
A: She wanted to see a butterfly.

12

Q; The man was hit in the head with a can of Sprite.
A: He's okay, it was a soft drink.

13

Q: Why can't you trust trees?
A: Because they are shady.

14

Q: What days do fish dislike the most?
A: Fry-Days!

15

Q: What did the guy say to the man who cut off his feet?
A: Oh no, you've defeeted me!

Dad Jokes

16

Q: Can February March?
A: No, but April May.

17

Q; Why was the cellphone wearing glasses?
A: Because he lost all his contacts.

18

Q: What did one plate say to the other?
A: Lunch is on me.

19

Q: What do you call a sad cup of coffee?
A: Depresso.

20

Q: What is the slipperiest country
in the world?
A: Greece!

Dad Jokes

21

Q: Why can't pirates finish the alphabet?
A: Because they got lost at C!

22

Q; What do you call a cow in an earthquake?
A: A milkshake.

23

Q: Why was the king only a foot tall?
A: He was a ruler.

24

Q: Why can't you trust atoms?
A: Because they make up everything!

25

Q: Why doesn't Pac-Man use Twitter?
A: He doesn't like being followed.

Dad Jokes

26

Q: What do we call a crying sister?
A: A crisis.

27

Q; If you ever get cold, just stand in a corner for a bit.
A: They're usually 90 degrees.

28

Q: What do you call a shoe made from a banana?
A: A slipper.

29

Q: Why didn't the skeleton cross the road?
A: He didn't have the guts.

30

Q: Why do seagulls live by the sea?
A: Because if they lived by the bay they'd be bagels!

Dad Jokes

31

Q: Why did the baker stop making doughnuts?
A: He got tired of the hole thing!

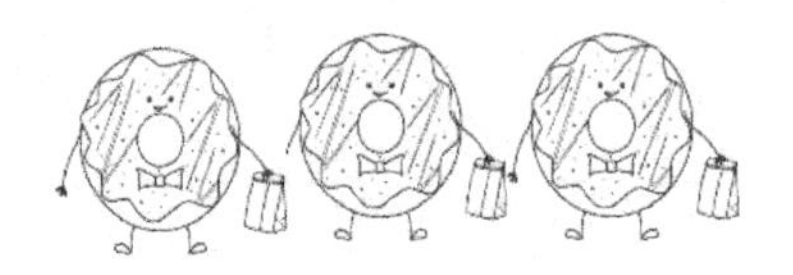

32

Q; Why you can't hear the Pterodactyl go to the bathroom?
A: Because the "P" is silent.

33

Q: Why was Cinderella kicked off the softball team?
A: Because she kept running from the ball.

34

I have a lot of good jokes about unemployed people... But none of them work.

35

Message to the people who created the number zero:
Thanks for nothing!

Dad Jokes

36

Q: What did the buffalo say to his son
when he left for college?
A: Bison.

37

Q: What do you call an alligator
that reads maps?
A: A navigator.

38

Q: What's the best thing
about living in Switzerland?
A: I don't know, but the flag is a big plus!

39

My boss told me to have a good day.
So I went home.

40

My mom told me to follow my dreams,
so I went back to sleep.

Dad Jokes

41

Q: What do you call a fake noodle?
A: An impasta!

42

Q: What did the vegetables say at the party?
A: Lettuce turnip the beet!

43

Q: What do a baseball team and a pancake have in common?
A: They both need a good batter.

44

Q: What did Barack Obama say to Michelle when he proposed?
A: I don't wanna be Obama self.

45

Q: How does Moses make his tea?
A: Hebrews it.

Dad Jokes

46

Q: What do you call a dinosaur with
an extensive vocabulary?
A: A thesaurus.

47

I sent ten puns to my friend hoping that they would make him laugh. But no pun in ten did.

48

I had a fear of speed bumps,
but I'm slowly getting over it.

49

Q: Did you hear about the kidnapping at school!?
A: It's okay. He woke up.

50

Q: What do you call a bear with no teeth?
A: A gummy bear.

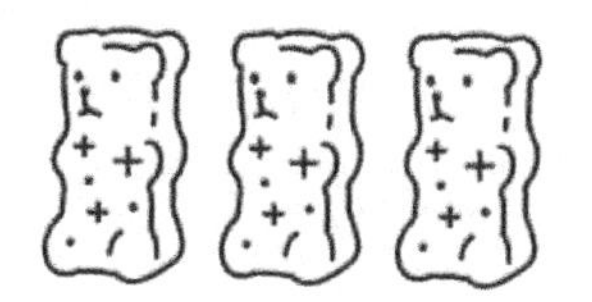

Dad Jokes

51

Q: What happens if you eat yeast
and shoe polish?
A: Every morning you rise and shine.

52

Q: What do you call a boomerang
that doesn't come back?
A: A stick.

53

I tried to catch some Fog. I mist.

54

Some people have difficulties sleeping,
but I can do it with my eyes closed.

55

Q: Can a kangaroo jump higher than
the empire state building?
A: Of course it can, the empire state
building can't jump!

Dad Jokes

56

Q: Did you hear about the guy whose whole left side was cut off?
A: He's all right now.

57

Q: How would you split the Roman Empire in half?
A: With a pair of Caesars.

58

Q: What do eggs do for fun?
A: karyolkie

59

Q: What is a tornado's favorite game?
A: TWISTER

60

Q: What do you call an apple thrown at your face?
A: A fruit punch.

Dad Jokes

61

Q: Which country does bacteria
like the most?
A: Germany.

62

Q: How did the flashlight feel
when his batteries died?
A: He was delighted!

63

Q: Why did the hipster fall in the lake?
A: He went ice skating before it was cool.

64

Q: Why don't cannibals eat clowns?
A: Because they taste funny.

65

Q: Don't you hate it when people answer
their own questions?
A: I do.

Dad Jokes

66

I used to be addicted to the Hokey Pokey,
but I turned myself around.

67

Q: Where was the treaty of Cape Town signed?
A: At the bottom of the page.

68

Q: What do you call a sleeping dinosaur?
A: A Dino-Snore

69

Q: What did the hat say to the tie?
A: You hang here, I'll go on a head!

70

Q: What do you call a broken angle?
A: A rektangle!

Dad Jokes

71

Q: What did one wall say to the other?
A: Meet you at the corner.

72

Need an ark?
I Noah guy.

73

Q: What's the difference between a bird and a fly?
A: A bird can fly but a fly can't bird.

74

Q: Why was the ant so confused?
A: Because all of his uncles were ants.

75

People are making apocalypse jokes like there's no tomorrow.

Dad Jokes

76

Q: What do you call a car that everyone can buy?
A: Afford

77

Q: Why couldn't the pirates play cards?
A: Because they were sitting on the deck!

78

Q: What did Mrs. Claus say to Santa when she looked up in the sky?
A: Looks like rain dear!

79

Q: What do you call it when a banana eats another banana?
A: Canabananalism

80

Q: Why do celebrities stay cool?
A: Because they have a lot of fans!

Dad Jokes

81

I don't always tell dad jokes,
but when I do, he laughs.

82

Q: Why did my friends wear sunglasses
when I got into the classroom?
A: Because I was a bright student.

83

Q: You wanna hear a joke about construction?
A: Wait... I'm still working on it.

84

Last night me and my girlfriend watched
three DVDs back to back.
Luckily I was the one facing the TV.

85

Q: Where do I keep all my dad jokes?
A: The dadabase.

Dad Jokes

86

Q: Why did the farmer name his pig ink?
A: Because he kept running out of the pen.

87

My physics teacher told me that
I have potential. Then he threw me off the roof.

88

Q: Did you hear about the two guys that
tried to steal a calendar?
A: They each got six months.

89

Q: Why did the physics teacher breakup
with the biology teacher?
A: Cause they had no chemistry.

90

Q: What do you call birds that stick together?
A: Velcrows!

Dad Jokes

91

Q: What kind of tree grows in your hand?
A: A palm tree!

92

Q: What does a clock do when it's hungry?
A: It goes back four seconds.

93

Q: Why does a chicken coop have 2 doors?
A: Because if it had 4 doors it would
be a chicken sedan.

94

Q: What path do crazy people take in the forest?
A: The psychopath.

95

Q: Why was the tricycle not in a relationship?
A: It's always the third wheel.

Dad Jokes

96

Q: What do you call cheese that hasn't been shredded yet?
A: Ungrateful.

97

I have a friend who can't eat cooked bread. She's lac-toast intolerant.

98

Q: Why wouldn't the shrimp share his treasure?
A: Because he was a little shellfish.

99

Q: What do you call a lost wolf?
A: A where-wolf!

100

I wondered why the baseball was getting bigger. Then it hit me.

Dad Jokes

101

Q: What did one eye say to the other?
A: Between you and me something smells.

102

Q: How does a train eat?
A: It goes "chew chew!"

103

Q: Have you ever heard of the band
146 Megabytes?
A: Of course not. They haven't had any gigs yet.

104

There's a fine line between a numerator
and a denominator.

105

Q: What do you call a priest that's
also a lawyer?
A: A father-in-law!

Dad Jokes

106

Q: What time was it when the elephant sat on the fence?
A: Time to get a new fence.

107

Q: What kind of PC can sing really great?
A: A Dell

108

I was wrongly fired from my job as a stage designer today. I left without making a scene.

109

I used to be addicted to soap, but I'm clean now.

110

Q: Did you hear about the light bulb party?
A: It was pretty lit.

Dad Jokes

111

Q: What do cats eat for breakfast?
A: Mice Krispies!

112

Without geometry life is pointless.

113

Q: Do you want to hear a long joke?
A: Jooooooooooooookkkkkkkkkeeeeeeeeee.

114

Q: What do you call a group of men
waiting to get a haircut?
A: A barbercue.

115

Doctor: Nurse, how is that little girl who
swallowed 10 quarters yesterday?
Nurse: no change yet.

Dad Jokes

116

Q: Why did the deer need braces?
A: Because he had buck teeth.

117

Q: What prize do you get for putting your phone on vibrate?
A: The no bell prize.

118

There's a new type of broom out - it's sweeping the nation!

119

Q: What is a cow's favorite music note?
A: A beef-flat.

120

Q: What do you call it when a dinosaur crashes a car?
A: Tyrannosaurus wrecks!

Dad Jokes

121

I just bought a thesaurus and when I got home, all the pages were blank.
I have no words to describe how angry I am.

122

The past, the present, and the future walked into a diner. It was tense.

123

Q: Why do scuba divers fall backwards into the water?
A: Because if they fell forwards they'd still be in the boat..

124

Q: Why couldn't the keyboard sleep?
A: Because it has 2 shifts.

125

Q: Why do people carry umbrellas?
A: Because umbrellas can't walk.

Dad Jokes

126

If one synchronized swimmer drowns,
do the rest have to drown too?

127

Q: Why did the scientist install
a knocker on his door?
A: He wanted to win the No-bell Prize!

128

Q: How did the telephone maker propose
to his girlfriend?
A: He gave her a ring.

129

6 out of 7 dwarfs aren't Happy.

130

Q: How do you cut the sea in half?
A: With a sea saw.

Dad Jokes

131

Q: Why was the girl staring at the carton of orange juice?
A: It said concentrate.

132

Q: Why do cemeteries have walls?
A: Because people are dying to get in!

133

Q: What kinds of mistakes are common in a blood bank?
A: Type-Os.

134

Q: What did the skunk say when the wind changed?
A: It's all coming back to me now.

135

Q: Did you hear about the restaurant on the moon?
A: Great food, but no atmosphere.

Dad Jokes

136

Q:What do you call a person without a body and a nose?
A: Nobody knows!

137

Q: What do you call a watch on a belt?
A: A waist of time!

138

I always wondered where the sun went at night -- this morning it dawned on me!

139

I cut my finger slicing cheese, but honestly I think I may have grater problems.

140

Q: What did the green grape say to the purple grape?
A: Breathe!

Dad Jokes

141

I used to be a banker, but I lost interest.

142

Q: How do you make an egg roll?
A: You push it.

143

Q: What is the definition of a good farmer?
A: A man outstanding in his field!

144

Q: How do you make seven even?
A: Remove the s!

145

Q: Why did I fail my history class?
A: Because my mom told me to forget the past!

Dad Jokes

146

Q: What did procrastination say to suspense?
A: Eh I'll tell you tomorrow.

147

Q: Why can't a nose be 12 inches?
A: Because that's one foot!

148

I just got electrocuted.
It hertz so bad, Watt do I do?

149

I have a boyfriend and he is in another nation.
Imagination.

150

Q: What does a Honda car say
while it's driving?
A: I'm Honda road!

Dad Jokes

151

I invented a new word today.
Plagiarism.

152

Q: How did Harry potter get down the hill?
A: He walked... JK Rowling.

153

I wrote a song about a tortilla.
Well actually, it's more of a wrap.

154

Q: Why do pancakes get healthier
when you stack them?
A: It becomes a balanced breakfast!

155

Q: What do you call a cow with no legs?
A: Ground beef.

Dad Jokes

156

I wasn't originally going to get a brain transplant, but then I changed my mind!

157

I would like to give a shout out to all the sidewalks for keeping me off the streets!

158

Q: What is the coldest letter?
A: C, because it's in the middle of ice.

159

Q: Why do actors break a leg?
A: Because every play needs a cast.

160

Q: Why was the broom late for the party?
A: Because it over swept.

Dad Jokes

161

Q: What do you call a cow with two legs missing?
A: Lean Beef

162

I have CDO. It's like OCD but the letters are in alphabetical order, LIKE THEY ARE SUPPOSED TO BE.

163

Q: What's green and fuzzy, has four legs, and would hurt you if it fell out of a tree?
A: A pool table!

164

My dog used to chase people on a bike. It got so bad I finally had to take his bike away.

165

I went to the store to find a camouflage jacket. I couldn't find one.

Dad Jokes

166

Person 1: Somebody said you sound like an owl.
Person 2: Who?!

167

Q: What did the tree say to autumn?
A: Leaf me alone.

168

Q: What do you get when you have 10 rabbits and they all take a step back?
A: A receding hare line.

169

I used to be addicted to soap, but I'm clean now.

170

I did a theatrical performance about puns. It was a play on words.

Dad Jokes

171

Q: What season is it when you are on a trampoline?
A: Spring time!

172

Q: What's a vampire's' favorite fruit?
A: A Neck-tarine!

173

Q: What did one pen say to the other?
A: You are incredible.

174

Q: What did the clock say to the hand can?
A: You give me a minute.

175

Q: Can a match box?
A: No but a tin can.

Dad Jokes

176

Q: Did you know Michael Jackson made wrote a movie?
A: It was a thriller....

177

Q: What did the traffic light say to the car?
A: Don't look. I'm about to change.

178

Q: Why cheetahs are bad at hide and seek?
A: They're always spotted.

179

Q: What do ghosts ride in amusement park?
A: Roller ghosters.

180

Parallel lines have so much in common it's a shame they'll never meet.

Dad Jokes

181

Q: What is a pig's favorite relative?
A: His oincle.

182

RIP boiling water.
You will be mist.

183

Q: What did one snowman say to the other?
A: Do you smell carrots?

184

Q: Do you know why you don't see elephants hiding in trees?
A: Because they're really good at it!

185

Q: How do you find Will Smith in the snow?
A: You search for fresh prints!

Dad Jokes

186

Q: Why does the cat get a drum set?
A: Because he loves purrcussion.

187

Q: Why can't a T-rex clap?
A: Because they are extinct!

188

Q: Why was 6 afraid of 7?
A: Because 7 8 9.

189

Q: What do you get if you divide the circumference of a pumpkin by its diameter?
A: Pumpkin Pi

190

Q: Why can't the keyboard get locked outside?
A: Because he always has his keys on him.

Dad Jokes

191

Q: Which side of a duck has more feathers?
A: The outside.

192

Q: What is the chemical formula for Holy Water?
A: H2OLY

193

My phone falls from the tallest building,
but didn't touch the ground?
Because my phone was in airplane mode.

194

Q: What do you call a snake that works
for government?
A: Civil serpent.

195

Q: What is at the end of a rainbow?
A: The letter W!

Dad Jokes

196

Q: What do you mean I'm not a bear?
A: I have all the koalafications.

197

A book fell on my head.
All I have to blame is my shelf.

198

Q: Why is Dracula so unpopular?
A: He's a pain in the neck.

199

Q: What two things can people not eat for breakfast?
A: Lunch and dinner.

200

Q: Did you hear about the light bulb party?
A: It was pretty lit.

Dad Jokes

201

"This is your captain speaking, AND THIS IS YOUR CAPTAIN SHOUTING."

202

Q: What did the number zero say to the number eight?
A: Your belt is too tight!

203

Q: What has a bottom at its top?
A: A leg.

204

Time flies like an arrow.
Fruit flies like a banana.

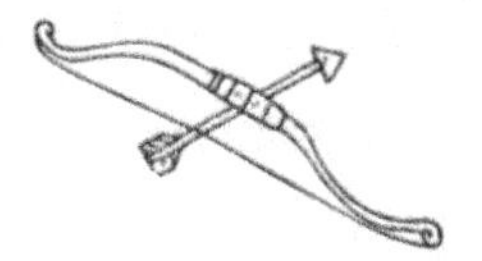

205

I was going to tell a dubstep joke, but I dropped it.

Dad Jokes

206

Q: What kind of bagel can fly?
A: A plain bagel.

207

They could make a pencil with erasers on both ends, but what would be the point?

208

Q: What is Poseidon's favorite chewing gum?
A: Trident.

209

I hate Russian Dolls.
They're so full of themselves.

210

Q: What did the baby corn say to the mamma corn?
A: Where's popcorn?

Dad Jokes

211

Q: Do you know where Russian milk comes from?
A: Moscow!

212

Q: What do you call a happy pepper?
A: A jolly-peno!

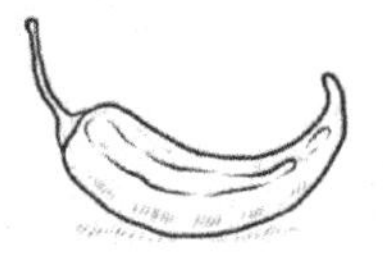

213

My grandfather would always talk about when the shovel was invented.
It was groundbreaking!

214

You know, people say they pick their nose, but I feel like I was just born with mine.

215

I found two heads of lettuce in my refrigerator.
The police have yet to find the bodies.

Dad Jokes

216

I tried Wookie meat for the first time.
It was Chewy.

217

Q: How did Sir Cumference get so round?
A: He ate too much pi!

218

I used to think air was free.
Then I bought a bag of chips.

219

Be kind to your dentist.
He has fillings too.

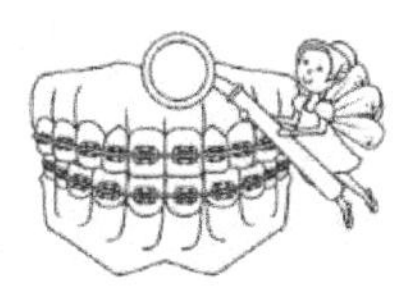

220

Q: Did you hear about the two skydivers that got married in the air?
A: They were falling in love.

Dad Jokes

221

Q: Why does Bernie Sanders drink skim milk?
A: He hates the one percent.

222

Q: How does a tree go on the computer?
A: It logs on!

223

Q: How do you organize a party in space?
A: You planet!

224

Q: What kind of dog doesn't bark?
A: A hush puppy!

225

Q: Where do sharks go on holiday?
A: Finland.

Dad Jokes

226

Q: How does the man in the moon cut his hair?
A: Eclipse it!

227

Q: How do you wake up Lady Gaga?
A: You poker face.

228

Q: What do you call a snake that's exactly 3.14 meters long?
A: A pi-thon.

229

I asked a scarecrow how he liked his job. He said, "It's not the best, but hay, its in my jeans!"

230

Q: Which flower talks the most?
A: Tulips, because they have two lips.

Dad Jokes

231

Q:How does a farmer count his cows?
A: By using a cow-culator.

232

Q: Why should you avoid people dressed as celery?
A: They could be stalking you!

233

I am now 22 years old and my eyesight is worsening. At what point do I get adult supervision?

234

Did you hear about the optometrist who fell into a lens grinder and made a spectacle of himself?

235

Q: Why did the coffee feel so upset?
A: He was mugged.

Dad Jokes

236

Q: How do parents punish their astronaut kids?
A: They ground them.

237

Q: What do you call a rich fish?
A: Goldfish!

238

Q: What did the elevator say about its job?
A: "It sometimes gets me down."

239

Q: How does a fish weigh itself?
A: By using its scales!

240

Q: Which is the coldest letter in alphabet?
A: B because it is in the middle of AC.

Dad Jokes

241

Q: How do you wash your clothes in the ocean?
A: With tide.

242

Q: What do you get if you cross a teacher with a vampire?
A: Lots of blood tests!

243

They laughed when I said I wanted to be a comedian - they're not laughing now.

244

Q: Why should you never iron a four-leaf clover?
A: Because you don't want to press your luck!

245

Q: What are a transformer's parents called?
A: Transparent.

Dad Jokes

246

Q: What did one math book say to the other?
A: Do you want to hear my problem?

247

Q: Where does the chemist wash his dishes?
A: In the Zinc.

248

A man just chased me with milk and cheese.
How dairy!

249

Two fish are in a tank. One turns to the other and says, "You man the guns, I'll drive."

250

Q: Why can't a bank keep a secret?
A: Because there are too many tellers.

Dad Jokes

251

Q: Why can't you borrow money
from a leprechaun?
A: Because they're always a little short.

252

I told my girlfriend her eyebrows were too high.
She looked surprised.

253

Q: What's orange and sounds like a parrot?
A: A carrot.

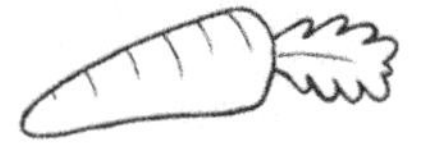

254

Q: Why did the police arrest the man levitating?
A: Because he broke the Laws of Physics.

255

Q: What are you gonna do in Rome?
A: Just gonna Rome around.

Dad Jokes

256

I can sympathies with batteries.
I am never included in anything either.

257

My girlfriend says I'm hopeless
at fixing appliances. Well she's in for a shock.

258

Q: What do you get when an elephant walks
through your garden?
A: Squash.

259

Dad, did you get a haircut?
No I got them all cut.

260

Q: What do you call a pig with three eyes?
A: A piiig!

Dad Jokes

261

Today a man asked for a small donation towards the local swimming pool.
I gave him a glass of water.

262

I'm a nobody, nobody is perfect, and therefore I am perfect.

263

A sandwich walks into a bar. The bartender says, "Sorry, we don't serve food in here".

264

Q: What do you call a Labrador that becomes a magician?
A: A Labracadabrador!

265

Q: Why did the bride cry at her wedding?
A: She didn't marry the best man.

Dad Jokes

266

Q: Why shouldn't you write with a broken pencil?
A: Because it's pointless.

267

Q: Why do cows have hooves instead of feet?
A: Because they lactose!

268

Q: What's Mario's favorite website?
A: Yahoo!

269

Q: Did you hear about the two baseball bats that were hitting on each other?
A: They were out of each other’s league.

270

Q: What was the coffees motto?
A: Espresso self.

Dad Jokes

271

I was going to walk down memory lane,
but I forgot.

272

Q: How did the French fry propose
to the hamburger?
A: He gave her an onion ring.

273

Q: Why did the dinosaur cross the road?
A: Because chickens hadn't been invented yet.

274

Q: Why is it hard to watch glass children?
A: Because they're always a pane!

275

Q: Why was the cook arrested?
A: Because he got caught beating an egg!

Dad Jokes

276

Q: Which electrical appliance has the least weight?
A: A light bulb!

277

Q: How do jail mates talk to each other?
A: They use "cell" phones.

278

Q: How did the barber win the race?
A: He knew a shortcut.

279

Q: What kind of music does a chiropractor listen to?
A: Hip-Pop!

280

Q: Why did the can crusher quit his job?
A: It was soda pressing!

Dad Jokes

281

Without dictionaries, life has no meaning.

282

Q: What did the cake say to the fork?
A: You want a piece of me?!

283

Q: Why did the chicken cross the road?
A: To prove he wasn't chicken.

284

Q: What do you call a kingdom with
a bored king?
A: Boredom.

285

Q: What is a fish’s worst day?
A: Fry-day.

Dad Jokes

286

Q: What ever happened to the guy who was afraid of hurdles?
A: He got over it.

287

If Apple made cars, would it have Windows?

288

Q: Why don't you use a dull pencil?
A: There's no point!

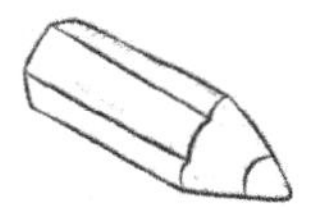

289

Q: Why does Snoop Dogg carry an umbrella?
A: Fo' drizzle.

290

Q: Why do bees have sticky hair?
A: Because they use honey combs!

Dad Jokes

291

Why did the lady sing lullabies to her purse?
A: Because she wanted a sleeping bag!

292

Q: What do you do when you see a spaceman?
A: Park your car, man!

293

Q: What did old soldiers used to eat
their dinner with?
A: Civil ware.

294

Q: What did one ship wreck say to another?
A: I've got a sinking feeling.

295

Q: Why do the birds sing??
A: Because they can't talk.

Dad Jokes

296

Q: What shoes do spies wear?
A: Sneakers.

297

Q: What do you call dinosaur eggs?
A: Eggxinct

298

Q: Did you hear about the guy who got hit by a can of soda?
A: He is alright now because it was a soft drink.

299

Q: Why do oranges hate the police?
A: They are always getting squeezed for information.

300

Q: Why did the orange stop in the middle of the road?
A: It ran out of juice.

Dad Jokes

301

Q: What gets wetter the more it dries?
A: A towel.

302

Q: What do jeans do to cool off in the summer?
A: They start panting.

303

Q: Why was the calendar famous?
A: Because he has a lots of dates.

304

A great app to use when you are in love is Candy CRUSH.

305

Q: What did the taxi driver ask the ware wolf?
A: Where wolf?

Dad Jokes

306

Q: What's Forrest Gump's password?
A: 1Forrest1

307

Q: Where did the basketball player get his doughnuts from?
A: Dunkin' Donuts.

308

Q: Why are horses so calm under pressure?
A: Because they come from a stable environment!

309

I'm on a seafood diet.
Every time I see food I eat it.

310

Q: What do you do with a sick boat?
A: Take it to the doc!

Dad Jokes

311

Q: What has 30 feet and horns?
A: The school band.

312

Q: Why did the banana go to the hospital?
A: Because he wasn't peeling so well.

313

Q: What did the science teacher climb?
A: A chemis-tree!

314

Q: What did the frog order for its dinner?
A: French flies and diet croak.

315

Q: Why did the sheep go to jail?
A: He was baaad.

Dad Jokes

316

Q: Why did Timmy hate eating clocks?
A: It was really time consuming.

317

Q: What do sprinters eat before a race?
A: Nothing! They fast!

318

Q: What do you call an alligator in a vest?
A: An investigator.

319

Q: What do you call an old snowman?
A: Water.

320

A USB and Flash are sitting in a car.
What did the USB say?
Flash, drive!

Dad Jokes

321

Q: What do you get when you cross a tyrannosaurus rex with fireworks?
A: DINO-MITE!

322

Q: What keeps your pants up in space?
A: An asteroid belt.

323

Q: Why are ghost's good cheerleaders?
A: They have a lot of spirit.

324

Q: What goes ooo ooo ooo?
A: A cow with no lips!

325

Q: What do you call a 3 legged donkey?
A: A wonkey.

Dad Jokes

326

Q: What kind of food gets put in the dumpster?
A: Junk food.

327

Q: What did the wave say when it fell?
A: "It hertz."

328

Q: Why did the scarecrow win an award?
A: Because he was outstanding in his field.

329

Q: What did the skeleton bring to the BBQ?
A: Extra ribs.

330

Q: How did the burger introduce his girlfriend to his family?
A: "Meat Patty."

Dad Jokes

331

Q: What did one hammer say to the other hammer when it did a good job?
A: You nailed it!

332

Q: What is a computer's favorite snack?
A: Microchips.

333

Q: Why is it so hard to play poker in the jungle?
A: Because there are so many cheetahs.

334

Q: What is a seal’s favorite subject?
A: Art art art art!

335

Q: Why will trump ban all shredded cheese if he's elected?
A: Because he is going to make America grate again!

Dad Jokes

336

Q: Do you want to hear an economics joke?
A: Never mind it's low on demand.

337

Q: Where does bad light go?
A: Prism.

338

Q: Why did Santa go to college to get a music degree?
A: So he could improve his wrapping!

339

Q: What is a mummy's favorite music?
A: Wrap music.

340

Q: How do you organize your nails?
A: You file them.

Dad Jokes

341

Q: How do monsters like their eggs?
A: Terri-fried!

342

Q: What do you call a girl standing under a roof?
A: Misunderstanding.

343

Q: What do cops eat for dessert?
A: Copcakes

344

Q: What did the salad say to her son yesterday morning?
A: "Get dressed."

345

Q: What do cows love to read?
A: The moospaper!

Dad Jokes

346

You wanna hear a joke about sheep?
Never mind its baaad.

347

Q: What's a lion and a witch doing
in a wardrobe?
A: It's Narnia business.

348

Q: What did the daddy water bottle say
to the baby water bottle?
A: Come here, squirt!

349

Q: What kind of music do wind turbines like?
A: They're heavy metal fans.

350

Q: What has 3 feet and can't walk?
A: A yard.

Dad Jokes

351

Q: How do you make a tissue dance?
A: You put a little boogie in it.

352

I'd tell you a chemistry joke but
I know I wouldn't get a reaction.

353

Q: Why doesn't Voldemort have glasses?
A: Nobody nose.

354

Q: Why did the squid cross the ocean?
A: To get to the other tide.

355

When knives were first invented,
they were cutting edge technology.

Dad Jokes

356

Q: What is a rock group with four members that don't sing?
A: Mount Rushmore!

357

Q: What does a cow do when his pals are on vacations?
A: Call his udder friends!

358

Algebra is x-sighting.

359

Q: What do you call zebras who are best friends?
A: Zebros!

360

As a wizard I like turning things into glass, I just wanted to make that clear.

Dad Jokes

361

Q: How long does it take to slip on a banana peel?
A: A banano-second.

362

Q: Why don't Americans like knock knock jokes?
A: Because freedom rings!

363

My therapist says I have a preoccupation with vengeance. We'll see about that.

364

Q: What do you call two guys that hang out above a window?
A: Kurt and Rod.

365

I entered ten puns into a contest to see which one would win. No pun in ten did.

Dad Jokes

366

Q: Did you know that milk is also the fastest liquid on earth?
A: It's pasteurized before you even see it!

367

Q: What do you call a pop star who makes honey?
A: Bee-yonce!

368

Q: What did the lemon say to the egg?
A:Egg-squeeze me.

369

Q: What do you call a sleeping dinosaur?
A: A dino-snore.

370

Q: How many tickles does it take to make an octopus laugh?
A: Ten tickles!

Dad Jokes

371

Q: How much do pirate earrings cost?
A: A-buck-an-ear!

372

I don't trust these stairs because
they're always up to something.

373

Q: What do elves learn in kindergarten?
A: The elf-abet!

374

Q: Why did the boy sleep under the oil truck?
A: To get up oily in the morning.

375

Q: What's red and smells like blue paint?
A: Red paint.

Dad Jokes

376

Q: How do teacups count?
A: Thir-tea-eight, thir-tea-nine, four-tea!

377

Q: What does a computer chip call its father?
A: Da-da.

378

Q: What do you call a suit that is burning in flames?
A: A blazer.

379

Q: What did the tomato say to the other tomato in a race?
A: Ketchup

380

Q: What is the difference between a snowman and a snowwoman?
A: Snowballs!

Dad Jokes

381

Q: Why did the teacher wear sunglasses to the school?
A: Coz the students were very bright

382

Q: Why did the turtle cross the road?
A: To get to the Shell station.

383

You blew up your Chemistry experiment? It's OK, oxidants happen.

384

Q: Why does Ed Sheeran not have a girlfriend?
A: Because she ran.

385

Q: If your nose runs and your feet smell what is wrong with you?
A: You're upside down.

Dad Jokes

386

Q: What did the bowl say to her child?
A: Be responsi-bowl.

387

Q: Wanna hear a joke about time?
A: I'll tell you later.

388

Q: Why do calendars always pay for their dates?
A: Because it's on them.

389

Q: What should you do if you break your toe?
A: Call a toe truck!

390

Q: How do you catch a squirrel?
A: You climb up a tree and act like a nut!

Dad Jokes

391

Q: What has 30 feet and horns?
A: The school band.

392

Q: Why did the banana go to the hospital?
A: Because he wasn't peeling so well.

393

Q: What did the science teacher climb?
A: A chemis-tree!

394

Q: What did the frog order for its dinner?
A: French flies and diet croak.

395

Q: Why did the sheep go to jail?
A: He was baaad.

Dad Jokes

396

Q: What do you call a boomerang that doesn't come back?
A: A stick.

397

Q: Why are empty math books always angry?
A: They have so many unanswered questions.

398

Q: What do noses say instead of goodbye?
A: Smell you later!

399

Q: How many apples grow on a tree?
A: All of them.

400

Q: What do call a cat when it eats a lemon?
A: A sourpuss.

Dad Jokes

401

Q: What do you call a pig who can do karate?
A: Pork chop!

402

Q: What was T-Rex's favorite number?
A: Ate!

403

Q: What did the cat say after eating two robins lying in the sun?
A: I just love baskin' robins.

404

Q: What makes a salad a salad?
A: Lettuce think about it.

405

Q: Where did the chicken go for vacation?
A: New Yolk!

Dad Jokes

406

Q: Why was the doctor angry when his assistant picked up a stick of butter?
A: He did not want them to spread it.

407

Q: What's a cracker's favorite band?
A: Panic! at Nabisco.

408

Q: Why couldn't the salad sleep?
A: Because it tossed.

409

Q: What is a DJ's favorite food?
A: Beets!

410

Q: Which item is the most indestructible in the avengers?
A: Hulk's pants.

Dad Jokes

411

Q: I just went to an emotional wedding.
A: Even the cake was in tears.

412

Q: What do you call a pile of cats?
A: A meow-ntain.

413

Q: What do you call a bee who is having a bad hair day?
A: A frisbee!

414

Q: Which country eats the unhealthiest food?
A: Greece.

415

Q: Why are horses the best dancing farm animals?
A: Because they know how to neigh-neigh!

Dad Jokes

416

Q: What do you call a sheep with no legs?
A: A cloud.

417

Q: Do you know what's odd?
A: Numbers that are not evenly divisible by 2.

418

Average people are mean.

419

Q: What cheese can never be yours?
A: Nacho cheese.

420

A rectangle hurt his side today.
His angles are all right though.

Dad Jokes

421

I quit my job at the herb garden because there was too much over thyme.

422

Q: Why do cows wear bells?
A: Their horns don't work.

423

Q: What did the letter say to the stamp?
A: Stick with me and you'll go places.

424

Q: What did the triangle say to the circle?
A: You have no point.

425

Q: What do you call your favorite ghost?
A: Your BOO!

Dad Jokes

426

Q: Want to hear a joke about a cookie?
A: Naaa, it's too crummy!

427

The astronomers got tired waiting for the earth to revolve around the sun.
So they called it a day.

428

Q: What did the acorn say when he grew up?
A: Geometry!

429

Q: What kind of shorts do clouds wear?
A: Thunder wear.

430

I just saw the world's worst thesaurus.
Not only was it awful, it was awful.

Dad Jokes

431

Q: Where did the kittens go on a class trip?
A: To the meow-seum.

432

Q: Why did the student eat his homework?
A: Because the teacher said it was
a piece of a cake.

433

Q: What is the difference between
an apple and an orange?
A: An orange is orange in color,
but an apple is not apple in color.

434

Q: Why did the frog always like to hang
out with the mushroom?
A: Because he was a fungi to be with.

435

Q: What's Irish and stays out all night?
A: Paddy o'furniture.

Dad Jokes

436

I asked for coffee at an alphabet cafe,
but they gave me a cup of T, instead.

437

Q: What do you call a moose obsessed with long term, committed relationships?
A: Monogamoose.

438

Q: Why should you never mess with Post-Its?
A: They always stick together.

439

Q: What did the grandma cat say to her grandson when she saw him slouching?
A: You need to pay more attention to my pawsture.

440

Q: Why am I your calculator?
A: Because you can count on me.

Dad Jokes

441

Q: What is the largest ant on earth?
A: Antarctica

442

Q: Why did the skeleton not go to the Party?
A: Because he had no-body to go with him

443

My mom told me a secret,
then I spilled the beans.
It took me an hour to clean up.

444

My friend David lost his ID.
Now I call him DAV.

445

Q: What do you call a famous turtle?
A: A shellebrity.

Dad Jokes

446

Q: Which snake can help you clean your car windshield?
A: A viper

447

Q: Why did the dinosaur cross the road?
A: Because chickens were not invented

448

Q: What is the tallest building in the world?
A: The library because it has many stories.

449

You may not like my skeleton jokes...
But I found them humerus!

450

Q: What can you roll but never drop?
A: Your eyes.

Dad Jokes

451

I had a job at the IRS.
It was pretty taxing.

452

Dry erase boards are remarkable.

453

Q: Where do you store corn?
A: In a corntainer.

454

Q: What do you call a hippo with a runny nose?
A: A hipposnotamus.

455

Q: What did the bee say to the sushi store?
A: Wasa-bee!

Dad Jokes

456

Q: What's at the end of the Great Barrier Reef?
A: The letter f!

457

Q: What do you call and educated fish?
A: Sofishticated.

458

I was going to tell a joke about pizza,
but it was too cheesy.

459

Q: What do you get when you cross a
Christmas tree and an iPad?
A: A pineapple.

460

Q: What do you call a composer
who makes honey?
A: Bee-thoven!

Dad Jokes

461

Q: What is a waffle?
A: A pancake with abs.

462

My boss told me to leave all my problems out the door so I told him to wait outside.

463

Q: Why was the ice cube so smart?
A: Because it had 32 degrees.

464

I asked my friend to pass me a chair.
She refused. So, what did I say?
Chairing is Caring.

465

Q: What's red and hurts your teeth?
A: A brick.

Dad Jokes

466

Does the five-second rule apply to soup? Please hurry.

467

Q: What did one shark say to the other while eating a clownfish?
A: This tastes funny.

468

They told me I had type A blood, but it was a Type O.

469

Q: What did the computer do when he got home?
A: He opened the windows.

470

Q: How many Indian food jokes do I have?
A: Naan.

Dad Jokes

471

Q: What do snowmen do on the weekend?
A: Just chill.

472

Q: What happened to the Hyundai that crashed into the tree?
A: The Hyundied.

473

Q: What kind of shoes does a thief wear?
A: Sneakers!

474

Q: Why was the bolt so clean?
A: It was put through the washer.

475

Patient: Doctor, I feel like a set of curtains.
Doctor: Pull yourself together then.

Dad Jokes

476

Q: What should you do when you see an onion ring?
A: Answer it!

477

Q: What does the ghost teacher say to the class?
A: Look at the board, I will go through it again.

478

Q: What starts with P, ends with E, and has lots of letters in between?
A: A post office.

479

Q: Who owns iHOP?
A: Apple.

480

Q: How can you make the number seven even?
A: Just remove the 's'!

Dad Jokes

481

Q: Why did the gum cross the road?
A: It was stuck on the chicken's foot.

482

Q: Where can you practice your bow & arrow shots?
A: At Target.

483

Q: What is the opposite of understand?
A: Undersit.

484

Q: What do you get when you cross a snowman and a vampire?
A: Frostbite.

485

Q: Why can't you surf on microwaves?
A: Because they're too small.

Dad Jokes

486

Q: Where do cows go in their free time?
A: The mooseum.

487

Q: Who was the most famous animal artist?
A: Pigasso!

488

Q: What's a tornado's favorite game?
A: Twister!

489

Q: What is it when you live in a bubble?
A: Unbelievebubble.

490

Q: Why did the cookie cry?
A: Because his father was a wafer so long!

Dad Jokes

491

Q: You know those people who make calendars?
A: They can never take a day off.

492

Q: Where does the sun go to drink coffee?
A: Starbucks

493

Q: Why did the robbers steal the bathtub?
A: Because they wanted to get a clean getaway!

494

Q: What do you call a fish with no eye?
A: Fsh

495

Q: What do you call a man with no arms and no legs playing in the leaves?
A: Russell.

Dad Jokes

496

Q: What did Nala say to Simba when he was walking too slow?
A: Mufasa!

497

Q: Why did the ice cream and milk become friends?
A: Because they wanted to shake things up!

498

Q: What do you call golfers having a good time?
A: A par tee!

499

I keep trying to lose weight but it always finds me.

500

Q: Why cheetah's like to go to the super market?
A: Because they like fast food.

Dad Jokes

501

Q: Why did the car stop?
A: Because it got tired.

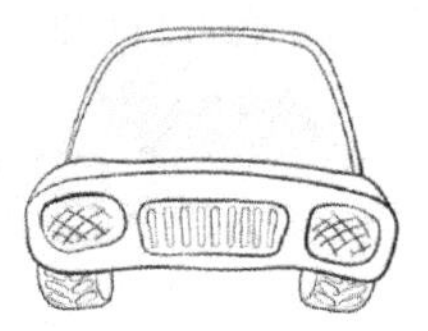

502

I think Windows are a pane.

503

Q: What do you call a robot dog?
A: A cybark!

504

Q: What did the farmer say when he lost his tractor?
A: "Where's my tractor?"

505

"I stand corrected", said the man in the orthopedic shoes.

506

Q: Where do lions live?
A: On mane street.

507

Q: How do you get an alien baby to sleep?
A: You rocket.

508

Q: Why is a swordfish's nose 11 inches long?
A: If it were 12 inches long it would be a foot.

509

Camping is intents!

510

Q: Why did the snake cross the road?
A: To get to the other sssssside!

Dad Jokes

511

Q: Why did the sales of battery go up in an area?
A: Because it was a remote area.

512

I've said it before, and I'll say it again.
I've said it before, and I'll say it again.

513

Q: When is a door not a door?
A: When it is ajar.

514

Q: What did the police officer say to his belly button?
A: "Freeze! You're under a vest!"

515

Q: Where do sheep get their hair cut?
A: At the baa-baa shop.

Dad Jokes

516

Q: What does a cow text with?
A: Emoooooojis!

517

Q: What did the mother bee say to her baby?
A: Beehive yourself!

518

Q: What do you call a can opener that doesn't work?
A: A can't opener.

519

Q: What do you call a computer floating in the ocean?
A: A Dell rolling in the deep.

520

Q: What do you call a laughing motorcycle?
A: A Yamahaha.

Dad Jokes

521

A woman thanked me on joining the vegetarian group.
But I've never seen herbivore.

522

Q: What do you call a funny mountain?
A: Hill-arious!

523

Q: What did the pirate say when he turned 80?
A: Aye matey!

524

Q: What tea do footballers drink?
A: Penal-tea!

525

Q: Who was the roundest knight at King Arthur's round table?
A: Sir Cumference.

Dad Jokes

526

Q: Why did the tree cross the road?
A: Because it was leafing.

527

Q: Did you hear the elevator joke?
A: It was wrong on so many levels.

528

My wife gets upset when I steal her kitchen utensils...But it's a whisk I'm willing to take!

529

Q: What can you put in a box that makes it lighter?
A: Holes.

530

Q: Why did the pie go to the dentist?
A: It needed a filling.

Dad Jokes

531

Q: How do you drown a hipster?
A: Just throw him in the mainstream.

532

Q: How much does a pirate pay for corn?
A: A buccaneer!

533

Q: What do you get when you cross a pig with a Christmas tree?
A: A porcupine.

534

A steak pun is a rare medium well done.

535

I made my password '14days' and it said it was two week to use.

Dad Jokes

536

Q: Did you hear about the little boy who was named after his father?
A: His name is Dad.

537

Q: Why can't you hear a Pterodactyl in the bathroom?
A: Because the P is silent!

538

Q: What do you call a sleeping bull?
A: A bull-dozer.

539

Q: What do you call a fast zombie?
A: A zoombie!

540

Q: What do fish put their money in?
A: A river bank.

Dad Jokes

541

Q: What do you call a bicycle
with popped tires?
A: A Popsicle.

542

Q: What do you call the head of the cups?
A: The Cuptain.

543

Q: Did you hear about the emotional tree?
A: It is such a sap!

544

Q: What is Bruce Lee's favorite drink?
A: Waaaattaaaaa!

545

Q: What did the rain droplet say when he was
ready to fall from the cloud?
A: Water we waiting for?

Dad Jokes

546

Q: What's a pirate's favorite exercise?
A: The plank.

547

Q: How rich are garbage men?
A: Filthy.

548

Q: Why did the brand manager post a clip of himself sneezing?
A: Because he wanted the video to get viral!

549

Q: What did the cat say to their owner?
A: You're purrrrrrrrrrrrfect!

550

Q: What does a janitor say when he jumps out of the closet?
A: Supplies!

Dad Jokes

551

Q: When is a car not a car?
A: When it turns into a driveway.

552

Q: What do you get if you cross Bambi with a ghost?
A: Bamboo!

553

Q: What did one ocean say to the other ocean?
A: Nothing. It just waved.

554

Q: Why did the chicken cross the playground?
A: To get to the other slide.

555

Q: Why can you never tell a kleptomaniac a pun?
A: Because they take things literally.

Dad Jokes

556

Q: When is a chef bad?
A: When he beats the eggs and whips the cream!

557

Velcro...what a rip-off.

558

Q: What do wasps take to feel healthy?
A: Vitamin bee.

559

Q: Why doesn't a bear wear socks?
A: Because he has bare feet!

560

I am terrified of elevators.
I'm going to start taking steps to avoid them.

Dad Jokes

561

Q: What do you call a sleeping werewolf?
A: An unaware wolf!

562

Q: Why is six afraid of seven?
A: Because there's something odd about him.

563

Q: What do cats do in their spare time?
A: They listen to meow-sic.

564

Q: Where does a horse go when it's injured?
A: To the horsepital!

565

Q: What is green and sits crying in the corner?
A: The incredible Sulk!

Dad Jokes

566

Q: What kind of car does an egg drive?
A Yolkswagen!

567

Q: What do you call two handbags running after each other?
A: A purse-uit.

568

Q: How do birds communicate?
A: They Twitter!

569

A boat carrying red paint & a boat carrying blue paint were in a collision.
The crews were marooned.

570

Q: Why did the chicken fall in the well?
A: He couldn't see that well.

Dad Jokes

571

Q: Why did the homeless guy drink only coffee?
A: He had no proper tea.

572

My son accused me of being immature.
I told him to get out of my fort!

573

A termite walks into a bar and asks
"Is the bar tender here?"

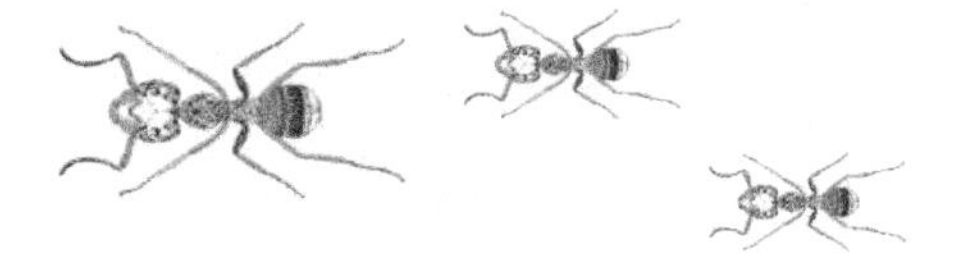

574

Q: Why was the scientists head all wet?
A: Because he had a brain storm!

575

Class trip to the Coca-Cola factory.
I hope there's no pop quiz.

Dad Jokes

576

I wanted to be a baker,
but I couldn't make the dough.

577

Q: Do you want to know something weird about the nervous system?
A: It's the most confident.

578

Q: Did you hear what happened to the guy who stole a calendar?
A: He got twelve months!

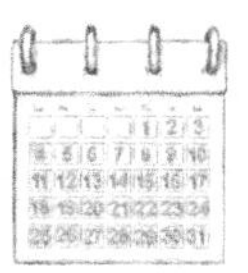

579

Q: Why couldn't the tree open his Facebook account?
A: Because he didn't know how to LOG in!

580

Q: How do NBA players stay cool during the playoffs?
A: They stand near the fans.

Dad Jokes

581

Q: What did one volcano say to the other?
A: I lava you.

582

I wanted to become a photographer,
but I lost focus!

583

An invisible man marries an invisible woman.
The kids were nothing to look at either.

584

Geology puns rock.

585

Q: What did the ground say to the dinosaur?
A: You made a big impression on me!

Dad Jokes

586

Q: How do you make a room warm?
A: By giving it a second coat.

587

My math teacher called me average.
How mean!

588

Q: What did summer say to spring?
A: "You're so last season!"

589

Q: What did a Nike shoe say to Adidas when he wanted to propose?
A: JUST DO IT!

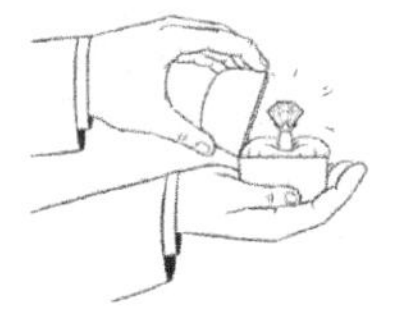

590

Q: Why is the obtuse angle always sad?
A: Because he is never right.

Dad Jokes

591

Q: What do you call underwear in a storm?
A: Thunderpants.

592

Q: What do you call a really nice human?
A: Mankind.

593

Q: What do you get if you cross a giraffe with a hedgehog?
A: A very long toothbrush.

594

Q: What do you call a bear with diabetes?
A: A gummy bear.

595

Q: How do you think the unthinkable?
A: With an itheberg!

Dad Jokes

596

Q: What do you get if you cross a van and an elephant?
A: A vehicle with extra trunk space.

597

Exit signs - they're on the way out.

598

Everything you've ever thought about was about potatoes or not about potatoes.

599

Q: What do you call a caveman who wanders aimlessly?
A: A mianderthall.

600

Q: What happens if you don't pay your exorcist?
A: You get repossessed!

Dad Jokes

601

Q: What did the teddy bear say after dinner?
A: I'm stuffed!

602

Q: Why do cellular biologists never agree with mathematicians?
A: For them, division and multiplication are the same thing.

603

Q: Why do bananas drag race?
A: They love to peel out!

604

Q: Why is a Calendar so popular?
A: Because he has to go to many dates.

605

Q: What kind of egg is bright on one side?
A: Sunny side up!

Dad Jokes

606

Q: What did the cow say to the fly?
A: Shooooo!

607

Two silkworms were in a race. Who won?
They ended up in a tye!

608

Q: Why do we tell the actors to break a leg?
A: Because every show has a cast.

609

Q: What did the ghost architect call his plans?
A: Boo-prints.

610

Q: Have you seen the Gravity book I brought?
A: I just can't seem to put it down.

Dad Jokes

611

Q: Why is Pavlov's hair so soft?
A: Classic conditioning.

612

Q: What did the mountain say to make the hill angry?
A: You are topless.

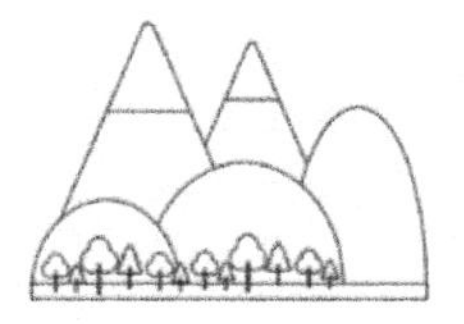

613

Argon walks into a bar, the bartender tells argon to get out. Argon doesn't react.

614

Q: Why don't aliens eat clowns?
A: Because they taste funny.

615

Q: What do you get when a book hits your head?
A: Facebook!

Dad Jokes

616

Q: Why didn't the flashlight get the joke?
A: It wasn't very bright.

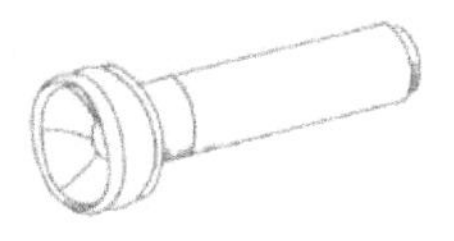

617

Q: Why did the football coach go to the bank?
A: To get his quarterback!

618

Q: What do you call a magic owl?
A: Hoodini!

619

Q: Why do cows eat from round hay bales?
A: Because they don't like to eat square meals!

620

Q: What do librarians take with them when they go fishing?
A: Bookworms!

Dad Jokes

621

I got fired from the frozen orange juice factory because I couldn't concentrate.

622

Q: Why is Bruno Mars so healthy?
A: Everyday 24 carrots!

623

I'm on a seafood diet. I see food and eat it.

624

Q: Where can you find the meaning of life?
A: On page 75 in the dictionary.

625

Q: What do you call a lonely piece of corn?
A: UNICORN!!

Dad Jokes

626

Q: What do you call a sleeping bull?
A: A bulldozer.

627

He threw sodium chloride at me!
That's a salt!

628

I told my doctor that I broke my arm in two places. He told me to stop going to those places.

629

Q: Why do hens lay eggs?
A: Because they can't throw them!

630

Q: Why didn't the guy mow his yard?
A: Cause he only had 2 feet!

Dad Jokes

631

Q: Why do bad farmers make terrible musicians?
A: Their beets are always bad.

632

I used to have a trampoline,
but it made me a little jumpy.

633

Q: What do you call a burning pocket?
A: A hot pocket!

634

Q: What do you call a dancing circle?
A: A polka dot.

635

Q: Why did the chicken cross the road?
A: To show the possum it could be done.

Dad Jokes

636

Q: What is worse than raining buckets?
A: Hailing taxis!

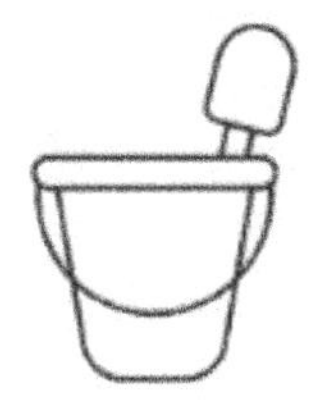

637

Geometry keeps you in shape.

638

Q: Why was the street expensive?
A: Because it wasn't the freeway.

639

I like angles to a degree.

640

Probability is chancy business.

Dad Jokes

641

Q: What did Apple order at McDonald's?
A: A Big Mac!

642

Q: What is the most delicious tower in the world?
A: The Leaning Tower of Pizza!

643

Q: Knock knock who's there Mikey!
Mikey who?
A: Mikey don't fit in the keyhole.

644

My friend's bakery burned down last night. Now his business is toast.

645

Q: What did George Washington say after crossing the Delaware?
A: Get out of the boat.

Dad Jokes

646

Q: Did you hear about the new restaurant on the moon?
A: The food is great, but there's just no atmosphere.

647

Q: What kind of currency do they have in space?
A: Starbucks!

648

Q: What did the British cereal say?
A: Cheerio!

649

Did you hear about the music note that flat out lied? It got in a lot of treble!

650

Q: What do you call a nosey pepper?
A: Jalapeño business.

Dad Jokes

651

Q: What does a golf course in the fall and a salad have in common?
A: They both have leafy greens.

652

Q: Which singer is fastest at stitching clothes?
A: Taylor Swift!

653

Q: How do you carve a tree?
A: Whittle by whittle.

654

Q: Why can't the sofa move by itself?
A: Because he doesn't have the money for an apartment.

655

Q: Why did two grapes leave another grape alone in the desert?
A: For no good raisin!

Dad Jokes

656

Q: Why didn't the melon run away to get married?
A: Because it cantaloupe!

657

Q: What pictures do turtles click?
A: Shellfies!

658

Q: What kind of keys can't unlock doors?
A: Monkeys!

659

Q: What should a person do when he has a lot of problems?
A: Open a mathematics book. It has many solutions!

660

Q: What game do astronauts play?
A: Moon-opoly!

Dad Jokes

661

Q: What does a toe do when it wants to move place to place?
A: It calls a toe-truck.

662

Q: How does a cow travel?
A: It MOOves.

663

Q: What do you call a person named Melissa?
A: Melissa!

664

Q: What did the man say to the belt?
A: You're a waist of time.

665

Q: What did the customer reply when the shopkeeper told him a bad joke?
A: "I'm not buying it."

Dad Jokes

666

Q: Why did the soccer player have so much trouble eating?
A: Because he thought that he couldn't use his hands.

667

Q: What did the bee say when he got home?
A: I'm back honey!

668

Q: What do you call 8 hobbits?
A: A hobbyte.

669

Q: How do you measure social media?
A: In Instagrams.

670

Q: Why was Cinderella bad at sports?
A: Because her coach was a pumpkin.

Dad Jokes

671

Q: What does a robot call his brother?
A: A bro-bot!

672

Q: Why couldn't the broken watch sleep?
A: It didn't have time!

673

Q: Why did the boy eat his sneakers?
A: He was in the mood for some fast food.

674

Q: Why did Mozart get rid of his chickens?
A: They kept saying bock bock!

675

Q: What did the pickle say to the pastrami after it told a dozen jokes?
A: You're on a roll today!

Dad Jokes

676

Q: Why did a worker eat an entire bag of sugar?
A: Because he was in a rush.

677

Q: Why did the tumbleweed cross the road?
A: It was windy!

678

Q: Why did mushroom go to party?
A: Because he Is a fungi.

679

Q: What's brown and sticky?
A: A stick.

680

Q: What kind of shoes do alligators wear?
A: Crocs.

Dad Jokes

681

Q: What does a dairy cow wear
when it plays basketball?
A: A jersey.

682

Q: What is the most uncomfortable of all birds?
A: The Wedgie-tailed eagle.

683

Q: Why to birds fly south for the winter?
A: Because it's too far to walk!

684

Q: What do you call a twin fruit?
A: Pears.

685

Q: Did I tell you the time I fell in love
during a backflip?
A: I was heels over head.

Dad Jokes

686

Q: Why are dinosaur bones so hard to carry?
A: They weigh a skele-ton!

687

Q: What's the difference between unlawful and illegal?
A: One is against the law the other is a sick bird.

688

Q: What did the cow say when it was caught in a traffic jam?
A: "Moove it!"

689

Q: What's a frog's favorite meal to order at the drive through?
A: French flies!

690

Q: Why do bananas put sunscreen on?
A: Because otherwise they would peel!

Dad Jokes

691

Q: What did one chimney say
to the other chimney?
A: Stop smoking.

692

Q: What's a porcupine's favorite plant?
A: A hedge-hog.

693

Q: Why does Voldemort use Facebook
and not Twitter?
A: Because he only has followers not friends.

694

Q: What did the Asus computer say
to the Lenovo keyboard?
A: Sorry. You're not my type.

695

Q: What did the bee say after getting home
from work?
A: "Honey, I'm home!"

Dad Jokes

696

Q: What do you call people in favor of tractors?
A: Protractors!

697

Q: How do billboards talk?
A: Sign language!

698

My water faucet fell out the window.
Yeah it hit the ground running.

699

Q: How do you catch a bunny?
A: You go behind a bush and make carrot noises.

700

Q: What is a pirate's favorite subject?
A: Arrrt.

Dad Jokes

701

The sign said READING IS NOT ALLOWED!
So I read my book quietly.

702

Q: Why did the snowman not stand
in the corner?
A: Because it was 90 degrees there!

703

Q: Why do you get into the pizza business?
A: To make some dough!

704

Sausage puns are the wurst.

705

Q: What do you call it when you put
Nutella on salmon?
A: Salmonella.

Dad Jokes

706

Q: What did the worker at the rubber band factory say when he lost his job?
A: Oh snap!

707

Always remember you are unique, just like everyone else.

708

Q: Why are frogs so happy?
A: They eat whatever bugs them!

709

Q: What do you call a pampered cow?
A: Spoiled milk.

710

Q: Why did the turkey cross the road?
A: It was the chicken's day off.

Dad Jokes

711

Q: What's at the end of the universe?
A: The letter e!

712

Q: Why do people always say
"brake a leg" to actors?
A: Because there is always a cast!

713

Q: How do spiders communicate?
A: Using the world wide web!

714

Q: If athletes get athlete's foot,
what do astronauts get?
A: Mistletoe!

715

A man didn't like his haircut, but it started to grow on him.

Dad Jokes

716

Q: Have you heard the one about
the corduroy pillow?
A: It's making headlines!

717

Slept like a log last night.
Woke up in the fireplace.

718

You can't run through a campground.
You can only ran, because it's past tents.

719

Q: What's the difference between a Hippo
and a Zippo lighter?
A: One is pretty heavy and the other
is a little lighter.

720

Q: Why the arena is always hot after an
NBA game is over?
A: Because all the fans have left!

Dad Jokes

721

Q: What's a frog's favorite drink?
A: Croaka-Cola!

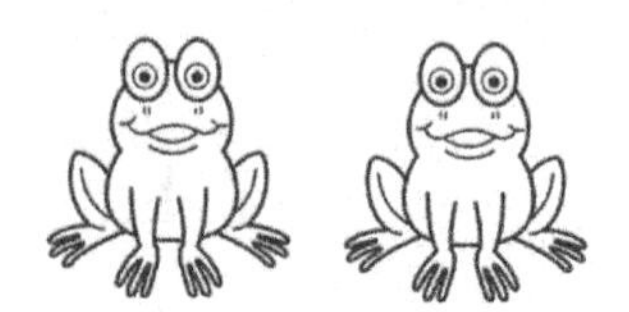

722

This belt is making me loopy.

723

Have some patience.
But I am not a Doctor.

724

Q: What did the dog say when he had to use the bathroom?
A: "Could you paws the movie, please?"

725

Q: Why is the Prime minister never seen in the morning?
A: Because he's PM, not AM!

Dad Jokes

726

Q: Why did the tree quit school?
A: He was stick of it!

727

Q: What did a pitcher say to the volcano?
A: Batter erupt!

728

Q: Want to hear something really cool?
A: Antarctica.

729

Q: What do you call icicles in spring?
A: Sprinkles!

730

Q: Why did the basketball leave the party?
A: It was ready to bounce!

Dad Jokes

731

Q: What did the bad driver say to the person he just ran into?
A: "My driving is hit or miss."

732

Q: What did the ocean say to the shore?
A: Nothing it just waved.

733

Mountains aren't just funny, they are hill areas.

734

Q: What do u call a girl with chillar?
A: Manushi chillar.

735

Q: What did the ear say when he was making announcements?
A: Ear ye,ear ye

Dad Jokes

736

Q: What did the wave say to the other wave?
A: Nothing, it just waved

737

Q: What did the hungry wall eat for lunch?
A: Wall nuts!

738

Q: What do you call a confused tree?
A: Stumped.

739

A magician was driving down the road and then he turned into a drive way!

740

Q: What do you get if you cross a firework and a chicken?
A: An egg-splosion!

Dad Jokes

741

Q: What has no legs but can do a split?
A: A banana!

742

Q: Why couldn't the shoes go out to play?
A: They were all tied up!

743

Q: What's a parasite?
A: Something you see in Paris.

744

Q: Why do some fish like to swim in salt water?
A: Because pepper makes them sneeze!

745

You're not my real ladder,
you're just my step ladder!

Dad Jokes

746

Q: Why did the Teddy bear turn down another slice of pie?
A: Because he was already stuffed!

747

Q: What did the hungry wolf say to the sheepdog?
A: Herd any lame ones, lately?

748

I got a new air conditioning system.
Yeah, I'm really not a fan.

749

Q: What do you call Garfield's uncle?
A: Garfuncle.

750

Q: What did captain Kirk find in the Enterprise's bathroom?
A: The captain's log.

Dad Jokes

751

Q: What's a bunnies favorite game?
A: Hopscotch!

752

Q: If big elephants have big trunks, what do small elephants have?
A: Suitcases.

753

Q: Why was the young horse always getting scolded?
A: Because he was always horsing around.

754

Q: What's a skeleton's favorite instrument?
A: The trombone!

755

Q: What did the glass of water say to the other glass?
A: Water you doing?

Dad Jokes

756

Q: Name a key that jumps around?
A: A monkey!

757

Q: Why is it hard for a ghost to tell a lie?
A: Because you can see right through it

758

I became a female construction workers
so I could pave the way for others to follow.

759

After multiple delays, the Encyclopedia of
Horology finally got published.
It's about time!

760

Q: Why is your nose in the middle of your face?
A: Because it is the scenter.

Dad Jokes

761

Q: Have you heard about the conversation of the peanut butter?
A: Actually, nah I shouldn't spread it.

762

Q: Wanna hear a joke?
A: Your life!

763

Q: What tea can turn into sweet and bitter?
A: Realitea!

764

Do not take life too seriously - you will never get out of it alive.

765

I once saw a car walking to an office in a suit. He definitely had the right a-tire!

Dad Jokes

766

Q: What kind of guns do bees use?
A: Beebee guns.

767

I wanted to learn how to drive a stick shift,
but I couldn't find a manual.

768

Q: Did you hear the story of the monkey?
A: It was a tall tail.

769

Q: If you don't live in Greenland and you don't live in Iceland, where do you live?
A: Neither land.

770

Q; What do you call a coin on top of spaghetti?
A: Penne pasta.

Dad Jokes

771

Q: What animal needs a wig?
A: A bald eagle!

772

Q: What is half burger kept in a freezer known as?
A: Ice berg.

773

Q: What kind of bag is not on the ground?
A: A Skybag!

774

Q: Why did the cow cross the road?
A: To get to the mooooooovies.

775

Q: Why did Mike fall off his bike?
A: Because he is a fish.

Dad Jokes

776

Q: Why does E.T. have such big eyes?
A: You would too if you saw his phone bill.

777

Q: What do you call a french man in sandals?
A: Phelipe Phalop.

778

Q: Why didn't the lifeguard save the hippy?
A: He was too far out, dude.

779

Q: What do you call a fake phone?
A: A Phoney.

780

Q: Why did the pig go into the kitchen?
A: He felt like bacon!

Dad Jokes

781

Two wastebaskets were trash talking each other. It was garbage.

782

Q: Why were the socks sitting in the fruit bowl?
A: They were a pair.

783

Q: What do you call a Pine tree that grows apples?
A: A Pineapple tree!

784

Q: Why do we drink water?
A: Because we can't eat it!

785

Q: How do you know when your dogwood trees are about to bloom?
A: When they bark!

Dad Jokes

786

Q: Did you hear about the guy who wears baggy pants?
A: Yeah it's in his genes!

787

Q: What do you call a waffle on a California beach?
A: A Sandy Eggo.

788

Q: What kind of fish can perform surgeries?
A: The sturgeon!

789

Q: When a lizard falls down, what will the other lizard say?
A: Tsk Tsk Tsk.

790

Q: Why did the web developer cross the road?
A: To GET to the other side.

Dad Jokes

791

Q: What is a penguin's favorite meal?
A: Icebergers.

792

You wanna hear a joke about memory!!!!!
Wait! I forgot my joke completely.

793

Q: Where does batman go to the bathroom?
A: The batroom.

794

Q: How do you know when you are going to drown in milk?
A: When it's past your eyes!

795

Q: What is sweet and lumpy?
A: Camelral

Dad Jokes

796

A skeleton walks into a bar and asks for a drink and a mop.

797

I was so shocked at my birth that I didn't speak for a good eight months!

798

Q: What time does the elf like to eat lunch?
A: Elfven o' clock!

799

Q: What did the chicken say after the musical?
A: That was eggcellent!

800

Q: What do you measure snakes in?
A: Inches because they have no feet!

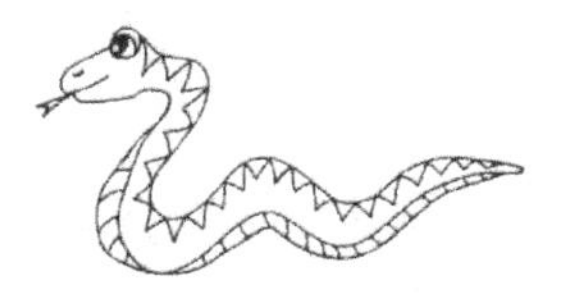

Dad Jokes

801

I was gonna tell you a joke about birds
but that'd be illegal.

802

Q: What did the proton say to
the grumpy electron?
A: Why so negative?

803

I can't wait until I'm 37.
I'll really be in my prime.

804

Two fish are in a tank. One says to the other,
"How do you drive this thing?"

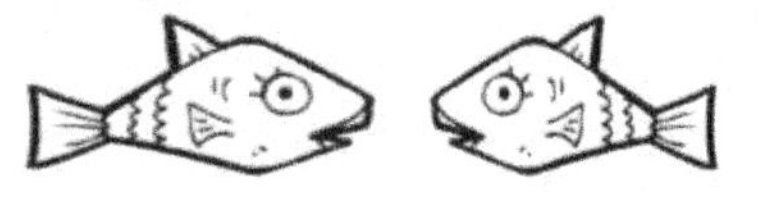

805

Q: What fruit loves everything?
A: Passion fruit.

Dad Jokes

806

Q: What did the snail say when it went piggyback riding on the turtle?
A: Weeeeee!

807

Q: What did you think of the Avengers movie?
A: It was quite the Marvel!

808

Q: How can you get online without the internet?
A: By standing on a line!

809

Q: Why don't birds follow directions?
A: They like to wing it.

810

Q: Why did the guy smear peanut butter on the road?
A: He figured it would go well with the traffic jam.

Dad Jokes

811

Q: Who keeps the ocean clean?
A: The mermaid.

812

Q: Why did the one handed man cross the road?
A: To get to the second hand store.

813

Q: Why couldn't the flower ride a bike?
A: The pedals fell off!

814

Q: How do you make an egg laugh?
A: Tell it a yolk.

815

Q: Who is a vampire likely to fall in love with?
A: The girl necks door.

Dad Jokes

816

Q: What vegetable sells like crazy?
A: Celery!

817

Q: What did one tree say to another?
A: I think I'm gonna go out on a limb here.

818

Q: What is a chicken's dream?
A: To cross the road without people questioning her motives.

819

Q: Why is a flower like the letter A?
A: Because a bee comes after it.

820

Q: Why shouldn't you listen to people who use sweeping generalizations?
A: Because they're all alike.

Dad Jokes

821

Q: Have you heard the one about the nearly perfect circle?
A: It's pretty well rounded.

822

Q: What did the ring say to the watch?
A: We're both very handy!

823

Q: What did Neptune say to Saturn?
A: Give me a ring sometime!

824

Q: What kind of tournament does a lamb love to take part in?
A: A champion"sheep"!

825

Q: Where do the vampires clean themselves?
A: In a bat-tub!

Dad Jokes

826

Q: Why does Wally wear stripes?
A: Because he doesn't want to be spotted.

827

Q: Why was the math book not feeling happy?
A: It had a lot of problems!

828

Q: Which country really needs the most food right now?
A: Hungary

829

I am Nike. You are McDonalds,
I am just doing it and you are loving it!

830

Q: Why aren't skeletons in the hall of fame?
A: No guts no glory!

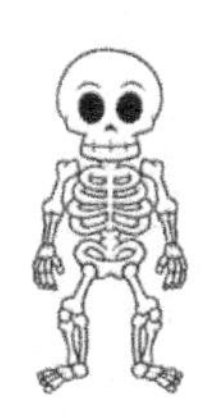

Dad Jokes

831

Q: I walked into a wall. Know what I saw?
A: Stars.

832

Q: What did the alien say to the librarian?
A: Take me to your reader.

833

Q: How did the seal react to a joke?
A: That's the sealliest joke I have ever heard.

834

Q: What do pigs use when they are hurt?
A: Oinkment

835

Q: What would a dog ask another dog for stopping?
A: 'PAW'se!

Dad Jokes

836

Q: What's the difference of a Tuna and a Guitar?
A: You can't Tune a fish.

837

A skeleton walks into a bar.
He goes up to the bartender and says,
"I'd like a beer and a mop."

838

I'm reading a book about anti-gravity.
It's impossible to put down.

839

Q: What do you call a person who farts in public?
A: A private tooter!

840

Q: How did the chicken dressed like Michael Jackson cross the road?
A: By doing the moon bwock!

Dad Jokes

841

A farmer in the field with his cows counted 196 of them, but when he rounded them up he had 200.

842

Q: How do you make time fly?
A: You throw it out the window!

843

Q: Why do ghouls and ghosts like to go in elevators?
A: Because they like to rise their spirits.

844

Q: What do you cut pizza with?
A: Little Caesars.

845

Q: What's an alligators favorite drink?
A: Gatorade.

Dad Jokes

846

A man walks into a bar.
He says, "Ouch!"

847

Q: Where does the Italian gangster live?
A: In the spaghetto!

848

Q: What's green and has wheels?
A: Grass. I was lying about the wheels.

849

Q: What does a Pikachu say when he's about to sneeze?
A: Pika-pika-achu!

850

Q: Why is the obtuse angle self-conscious?
A: Because it is not acute angle.

Dad Jokes

851

Q: What ship never sinks?
A: Friendship!

852

Q: What is nine's favorite sport?
A: Tennis.

853

Q: Where are eggs imported from?
A: New yolk.

854

Q: What did one lawyer say to the other lawyer?
A: We're both lawyers.

855

If I bought my balloon for $0.99, how much should I sell it for after adjusting for inflation?

Dad Jokes

856

Q: Are you from Tennessee?
A: Because you're the only ten I see.

857

Q: What did the ghost say to the wall?
A: "Hey, just passing through."

858

Q: What's the best time to go to the dentist?
A: Tooth-hurty.

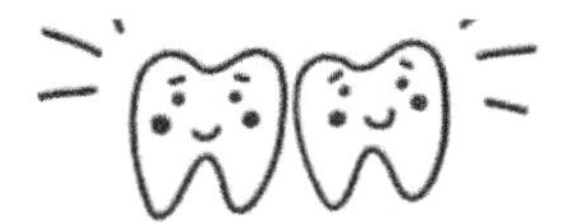

859

Today a girl said she recognized me from vegetarian club, but I'm sure I've never met herbivore.

860

Q: How does a firefly start the race?
A: On your mark. Get set. Glow!

Dad Jokes

861

Q: What kind of pants does Mario wear?
A: Denim! Denim! Denim!

862

Q: What do you call a psychic basketball player?
A: A crystal baller.

863

Q: What do you call it when you set a fern on a chair?
A: Furnichair!

864

Q: What do you call an alien with three eyes?
A: An aliiien.

865

Q: What do you get when you cross a pastry with a snake?
A: A pie-thon.

Dad Jokes

866

Q: How do bees get to school?
A: On a school buzz!

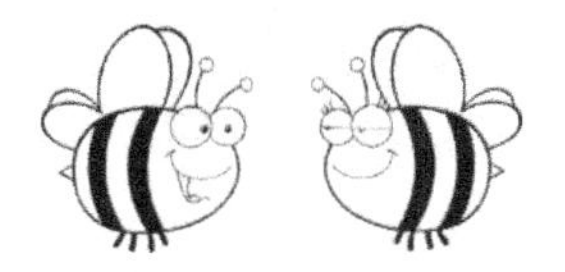

867

Fractions are chips off the whole block.

868

Q: What can you catch but not give away?
A: A cold.

869

Q: What do you call a bear trap after it's been put in the snow?
A: A brrrrrrr trap.

870

Q: Have you heard of the giant pickle?
A: It was a pretty big dill.

Dad Jokes

871

Q: What gate can never be opened?
A: Colgate!

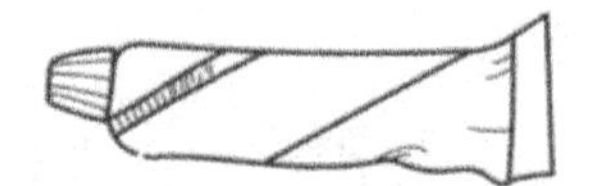

872

Q: What do you call a truck studying for semi-finals?
A: Nothing, trucks don't study for tests.

873

Q: Can I have a doughnut?
A: I doughnut think so.

874

A plateau is the highest form of flattery.

875

Are Samsung store security guards considered Guardians of the galaxy?

Dad Jokes

876

Q: How do you make a hot dog stand?
A: Take away its chair.

877

Q: What do you call a parrot that's missing?
A: A polygon.

878

Q: How do you punish your pet rock?
A: You hit rock bottom.

879

Q: What's the difference between
a piano and a tuna?
A: You can tuna piano but
you can't piano a tuna.

880

Q: What did the dad tomato say to his
slow son tomato?
A: Ketchup.

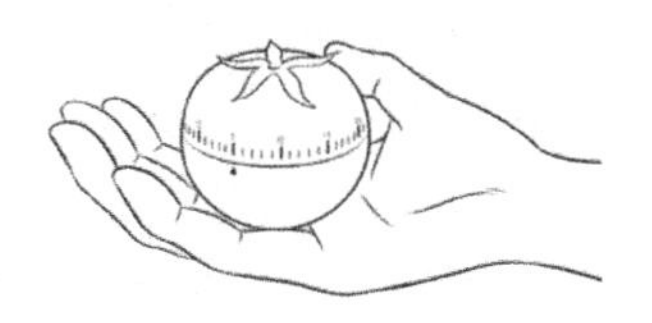

Dad Jokes

881

Q: What did the car say when it kept getting slammed?
A: Give me a brake!

882

Q: Why did Harry Potter not press the vol. button?
A: Because he was afraid Voldemort will be back again.

883

I have a pig, but it always goes ham.

884

Q: What's green and sings?
A: Elvis parsley.

885

Q: What did the bubble say when the other bubble popped?
A: Unbelibubble.

Dad Jokes

886

Q: What did the cat say after he told a joke?
A: I'm just kitten!

887

Q: What do you get if you copy a picture of a mallard?
A: A repro-duck-tion!

888

Q: How did the mummy get to class?
A: On the ghoul-bus!

889

Q: When do you stop at green and go at red?
A: When you're eating a watermelon!

890

Q: Why did the skeleton cross the road?
A: To get to the body shop.

Dad Jokes

891

Q: What did the mountain climber name his son?
A: Cliff.

892

I knew I shouldn't have eaten that seafood because now I feel a little eel.

893

Q: Why does it take longer to get from 1st to 2nd base, than it does to get from 2nd to 3rd base?
A: Because there's a Shortstop in between!

894

Q: Why was the mushroom happy?
A: Because he was a fungi.

895

Q: What do you get when two giraffes run into each other?
A: A giraffic jam.

Dad Jokes

896

Q: Why did the penny go to rehab?
A: Because he wanted to change!

897

Q: Why did the librarian never have free time?
A: All her time is booked!

898

Q: What does the elf like best in school?
A: The elfabet!

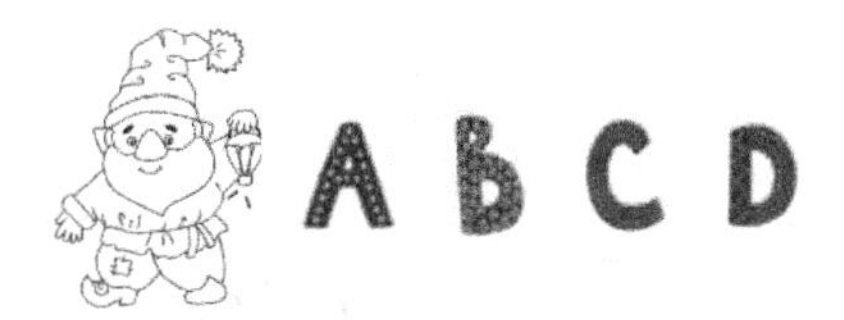

899

I just came back from a mind reader.
I just can't get her of my head.

900

Q: What do you call it when you cross a dinosaur and a pig?
A: Jurassic Pork.

Dad Jokes

901

Q: What did the stamp say to the envelope?
A: I'll stick with you.

902

Q: What do you call a mean hotdog?
A: A brat!

903

Q: What was Beethoven's favorite fruit?
A: Ba-na-na-na.

904

Q: Why was the Apple Store in Wilmington so afraid of competition?
A: They were Dell-aware.

905

Q: What shampoo does a doctor uses when there are no patients?
A: Clinic all clear.

Dad Jokes

906

Q: Why did Adele cross the road?
A: To say Hello from the other side.

907

Q: Why was the chicken afraid of the chicken?
A: It was chicken.

908

Q: What do you call a duck with a key?
A: Duckey.

909

Q: What did the cell say to her sister when she stepped on her toe?
A: Mitosis.

910

Q: What did A say to B?
A: C you tomorrow.

Dad Jokes

911

Q: What do you call the meanest steer in the pasture?
A: Beef jerky!

912

Q: What do you fix a tuba with?
A: A tuba glue.

913

Q: Why does the can cross the road?
A: Because he can!

914

Q: Why didn't Noah do any fishing while on the ark?
A: He only brought two worms!

915

Driving home, I was behind a Transformer tractor yesterday. It turned into a field.

Dad Jokes

916

Did you hear the joke about the jump rope?
Skip it.

917

Q: What is the favorite drink of cats?
A: Meow-tain dew!

918

Q: What did Yoda say on Valentine 's Day?
A: Yoda one for me.

919

Q: What transit system do pearls use?
A: Clamtrak.

920

Q: Where does Dustin put dust?
A: He puts the Dust-in, the trash

Dad Jokes

921

Q: Did you hear about the red ship and the blue ship that collided?
A: Both crews were marooned!

922

Q: What room can no one enter?
A: A mushroom!

923

Q: What do you call a grandmother who cracks jokes?
A: A Gram cracker!

924

Q: What time is it when ten elephants are chasing you?
A: Ten after one!

925

Q: How do you get a mouse to smile?
A: Say cheese!

Dad Jokes

926

I hate waking up.

927

Q: What does a vegan zombie eat?
A: Graaaaaaaaaaaaaaaaaaaaaains!

928

Q: What did the farmer say to the green pumpkin?
A: Why orange you orange?

929

Q: What did the cat say to the dog?
A: Why you gotta play so ruff?

930

Q: Where does George Washington keep his armies?
A: In his sleevies.

Dad Jokes

931

Q: What is the tallest building in the world?
A: The library - it has the most stories!

932

Q: Which is the heaviest noodle?
A: Wanton noodles.

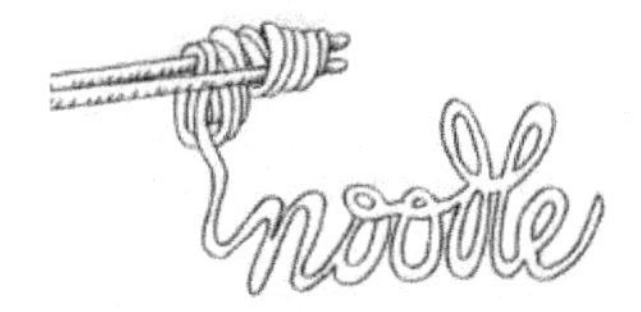

933

Q: What did the small pickle say to the big pickle that did bad on his test?
A: Don't worry, it's no big dill.

934

Division cuts me up!

935

Q: What's an angels favorite video game?
A: Halo!

Dad Jokes

936

Two guys walk into a bar.
The third guy ducks!

937

Your prairie dog hunting and you see one?
You just gotta gofer it!

938

Q: What is Mr. T's favorite month?
A: April, fools.

939

Q: If April showers bring May flowers,
what do May flowers bring?
A: Pilgrims.

940

Q: How do you tell the gender of an ant?
A: Drop it in water. If it sinks, girl ant.
If it floats, boy ant.

Dad Jokes

941

Q: Why was the letter P not in the alphabet?
A: L M NO P

942

Q: What do you call a girl who pushes her father from a cliff?
A: Push-pa!

943

Q: Why did the cowboy adopt a Dachshund?
A: To get a long little doggie!

944

Q: What did the ape order for lunch?
A: A gorilla-cheese sandwich.

945

Q: What do you say when you get carried away by a thousand balloons?
A: I must have gotten a little carried away.

Dad Jokes

946

Q: What do you call a laughing motorcycle?
A: A Hahahaharley.

947

Q: What's bread's favorite thing to do?
A: Loaf around!

948

I met an old guy talking to his coins.
What he says makes cents.

949

Q: What ended at the beginning of 1896?
A: 1895!

950

Q: Why did the cookie go to the hospital?
A: Because he felt crummy.

Dad Jokes

951

Q: Why is a Koala not a real bear?
A: It doesn't meet the koalafications!

952

Q: Why did the skeleton go to
the party alone?
A: He had no body to go with him!

953

I needed a password eight characters long
so I picked Snow White and the Seven Dwarfs.

954

Q: Where do leaves go to school?
A: Treeschool.

955

Q: What movie goes by really fast?
A: Rush Hour.

Dad Jokes

956

I used to work in a shoe recycling shop.
It was sole destroying.

957

How come boxers aren't good at comedy?
Their punchlines always knock people out.

958

Q: What is the worst kind of pie?
A: 3.1415

959

Q: Who is haldirams brother?
A: Haldilakshaman

960

Q: What is a bee that can sing and dance?
A: CardiB

Dad Jokes

961

Q: What's the karate expert's favorite beverage?
A: Kara-tea

962

Q: What does a frog use when it goes fishing?
A: A tadpole!

963

Q: Why don't stairs like mirrors?
A: No one likes being stared at.

964

Q: What's the difference between a suite and a regular hotel?
A: The suite tastes better.

965

I could go on and on and on and on about sequences.

Dad Jokes

966

Q: How did the chicken cross the road?
A: By "winging" it.

967

Q: What happens when Yoda becomes a toy?
A: It is now called Toyota!

968

Q: What happened to the plant in math class?
A: It grew square roots.

969

Q: What did the baby puffer fish say to his mom?
A: Where's pops?

970

Q; What do you call a potato that is wearing glasses?
A: A spectator!

Dad Jokes

971

Q: Why does a room full of married people looks so empty and deserted?
A: There's not even a "single person" in it.

972

Q: Why did the strawberry cross the road?
A: Because his mother was in a jam.

973

Q: What do you call two bodies of water that are enemies?
A: Arch neme-seas!

974

Q: What do you get when you cross a lion and a chicken?
A: A full lion.

975

Q: Why did Donald Trump go back to the store?
A: He forgot toupee.

Dad Jokes

976

Q: What do a monkey and a bicycle have in common?
A: They both have handlebars except for the monkey.

977

Q: What is a physicist's favorite food?
A: A Heisenburger!

978

Q: Why are fireflies like cars?
A: Because they both have taillights.

979

Q: What do you get if you cross a stereo and a refrigerator?
A: Very cool music.

980

Q: What is the robot teacher's favorite part of the day?
A: Assembly.

Dad Jokes

981

Q: What kind of chocolate is the best?
A: 5-Star, because they always have 5 stars.

982

Q: What did one boy car say to the other girl car?
A: You rev me up.

983

Q: Where do pencils go on vacation?
A: Pencilvania

984

Q: Why do the French eat snails?
A: Because they don’t like fast foods.

985

Q: What is a ghost's favorite game?
A: Peeka-boo!

Dad Jokes

986

Q: What side of the house do trees grow best on?
A: The outside!

987

Q: Are you breakfast?
A: Because you're bae-goals.

988

Q: What did the drum say when it fell down?
A: BA DUM TSHHHH!

989

Q: How does a cow greet a human?
A: Hay there.

990

Q: Why do the French only put one egg in an omelette?
A: Because one egg is un oeuf.

Dad Jokes

991

Q: How did the dentist become a brain surgeon?
A: His hand slipped.

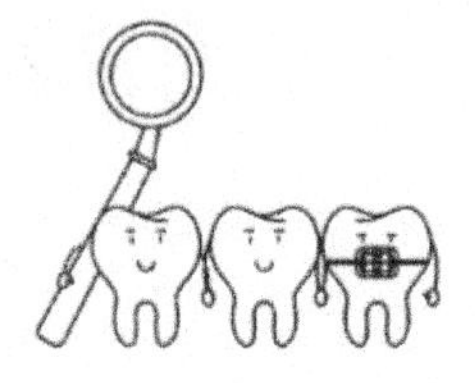

992

Q: How do you get Pikachu on the bus?
A: You Pokemon.

993

Q: What did the conceited worm say?
A: Chick's dig me.

994

I heard that Oxygen and Magnesium got together. OMg!

995

I would make another Chemistry joke, but all the good ones Argon.

Dad Jokes

996

Q: What's the biggest event of the year
for potatoes?
A: Starch Madness!

997

Q: How many lips does a flower have?
A: Tulips.

998

Q: What do you call an acid with an attitude?
A: A mean oh acid.

999

Q: What has 4 eyes but can't see anything?
A: Mississippi.

1000

Q: What did the solider sheep do?
A: He went AWOOL.

Congratulations for Making It to the End!

I won't make any claims but chances are that by now you're what I'd call a pun-master.

With you newfound talent for unfunny humor, I invite you to spread some fun to your friends, family, and just about anyone else!

People may not admit it but they all secretly love dad jokes. Trust me, I'm one of them!

Best-Selling Titles by the Author:

Would You Rather... For Kids and Their Adults! **365 Clean and Hilarious Questions the Entire Family Will Enjoy!**
http://bit.ly/WouldYouR

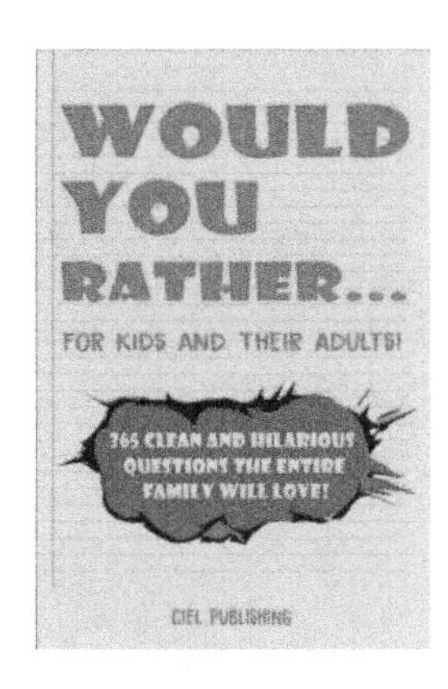

Rubik's Cube Solution Guide for Kids **(3x3x3 and 2x2x2) in Full Color**
http://bit.ly/Rubiks4Kids

Riddles for Kids: **365 Riddles for Daily Laughs and Giggles**
http://bit.ly/RiddlesKids

And lastly… If you liked this book, please leave a review!

Amazon reviews from our readers help us keep producing quality content. We're counting with yours!

Thanks!

Made in the USA
Coppell, TX
02 December 2020